SCIENTIFIC AMERICAN EDUCATIONAL PUBLISHING

SCIENTIFIC AMERICAN INVESTIGATES THE HUMAN BODY

THE DIGESTIVE SYSTEM

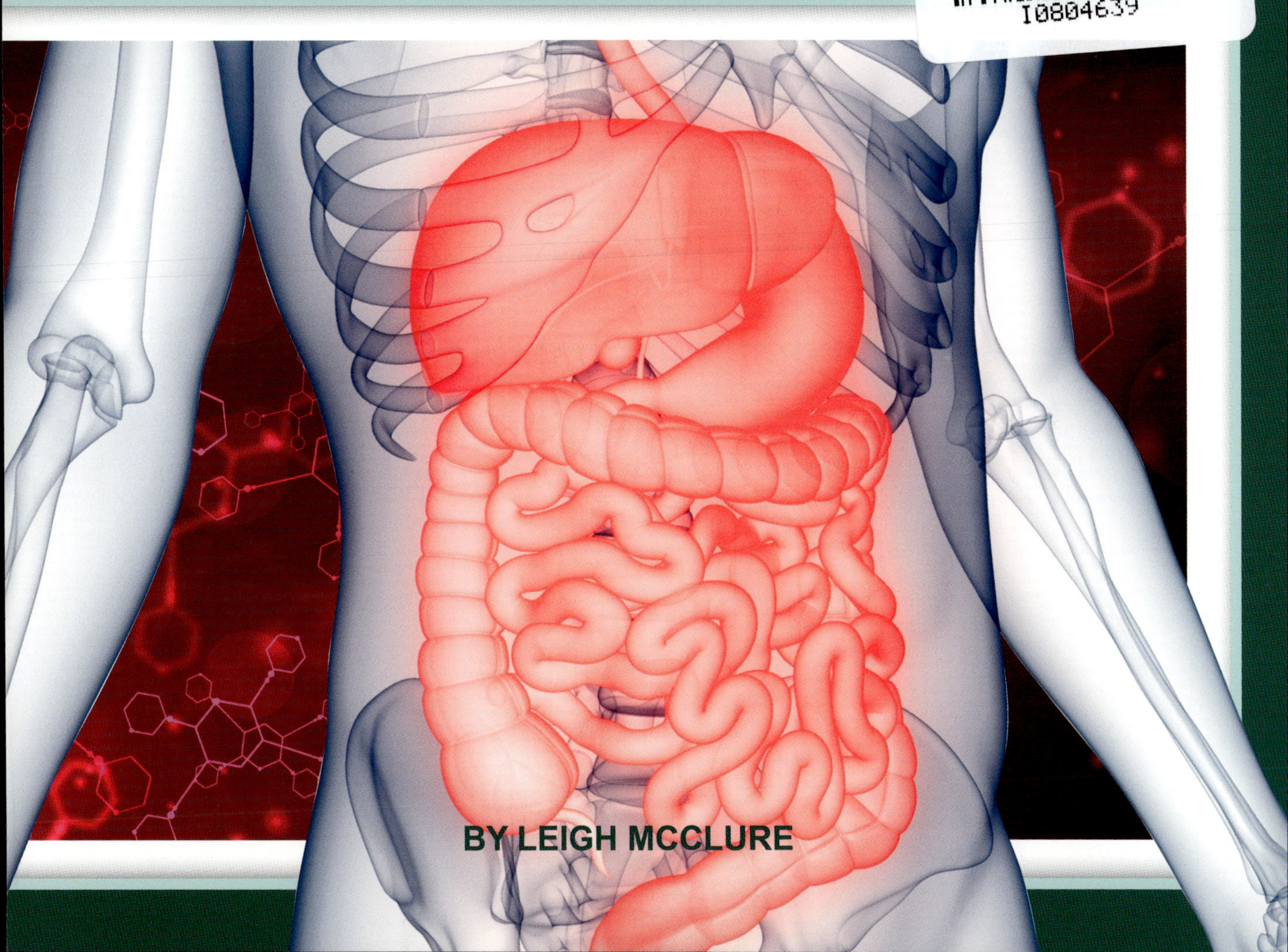

BY LEIGH MCCLURE

Published in 2025 by The Rosen Publishing Group
in association with Scientific American Educational Publishing
2544 Clinton Street, Buffalo NY 14224

Library of Congress Cataloging-in-Publication Data
Names: McClure, Leigh, author.
Title: The digestive system / Leigh McClure.
Description: Buffalo, NY : Scientific American Educational Publishing, [2025] | Series: Scientific American investigates the human body | Includes bibliographical references and index.
Identifiers: LCCN 2024011769 (print) | LCCN 2024011770 (ebook) | ISBN 9781725351394 (library binding) | ISBN 9781725351387 (paperback) | ISBN 9781725351400 (ebook)
Subjects: LCSH: Digestive organs–Juvenile literature. | Digestion–Juvenile literature. | Nutrition–Juvenile literature. | Human anatomy–Juvenile literature.
Classification: LCC QM301 .M33 2025 (print) | LCC QM301 (ebook) | DDC 612.3–dc23/eng/20240324
LC record available at https://lccn.loc.gov/2024011769
LC ebook record available at https://lccn.loc.gov/2024011770

Designer: Andrea Davison-Bartolotta
Editor: Caitlin McAneney

Portions of this work were originally authored by John M. Shea, MD, and published as *The Digestive System*. All new material in this edition authored by Leigh McClure.

Photo credits: Cover, p. 1 (main) Magic mine/Shutterstock.com; cover, p. 1 (background) jijomathaidesigners/Shutterstock.com; p. 5 NDAB Creativity/Shutterstock.com; p. 7 VictoriaArt/Shutterstock.com; p. 9 namaki/Shutterstock.com; p. 11 Marko Aliaksandr/Shutterstock.com; p. 13 Kateryna Kon/Shutterstock.com; p. 15 Tattoboo/Shutterstock.com; p. 17 Samuel Borges Photography/Shutterstock.com; p. 18 Monkey Business Images/Shutterstock.com; p. 19 VectorMine/Shutterstock.com; pp. 21, 29 Africa Studio/Shutterstock.com; p. 23 CGN089/Shutterstock.com; p. 25 ChameleonsEye/Shutterstock.com; p. 27 Anna_Pustynnikova/Shutterstock.com.

Printed in the United States of America

CPSIA compliance information: Batch #CSSA25. For Further Information contact Rosen Publishing at 1-800-237-9932.

CONTENTS

Words in the glossary appear in **bold** type the first time they are used in the text.

FUELING THE BODY

Why do we need to eat food every day? Where does the food go? How does the body use it? All of these questions have to do with the digestive system. Exploring the digestive system can help you understand how the nutrients we take in fuel our bodies.

The human body needs nutrients to keep it running. Certain foods provide special nutrients to the body. Think of the last thing you ate. That food has nutrients that are now helping your body function, or work as it's supposed to. To be able to use nutrients, the body must first break foods down into smaller parts. Digestion is the process of breaking down food into useful nutrients. Let's explore the digestive system!

FUN FACT

SOME LIVING THINGS, SUCH AS PLANTS, MAKE THEIR OWN FOOD FROM SUNLIGHT. OTHER CREATURES, SUCH AS EXTREMELY SMALL **BACTERIA**, ONLY NEED A TINY AMOUNT OF NUTRIENTS TO GROW.

Fresh foods like fruits and vegetables can give your body many nutrients.

A Journey Through the System

Imagine the digestive system as one long tract, or tube. It starts with the mouth, where we put food in, and ends with the anus, where waste leaves our bodies. Every part of the digestive system has a specific job to help us get the most nutrients from our food. Most jobs involve breaking down food and moving nutrients from the digestive tract to the bloodstream.

ESSENTIAL NUTRIENTS

What you eat plays a special part in your overall health. Carbohydrates, which include sugars and **starches**, are the body's main source of energy. Proteins—which are made up of smaller chemicals called amino acids—are the basic building blocks for the human body. Lipids, sometimes known as fats, are made from smaller chemicals called fatty acids. While many people think that all fats are bad for you, some types, such as omega-3 found in fish and other foods, are necessary to prevent some diseases.

Water is an important nutrient. More than half of our body is made of water. We need to drink enough every day to help keep our bodies well **hydrated**. Some doctors recommend you drink the same number of 8-ounce (237 ml) glasses a day as your age, up to age eight.

Healthy fats, found in foods like eggs and avocado, are important for both growth and energy.

Minerals Matter

Minerals are found in foods you eat. Minerals are nutrients that plants take in from the soil. The human body needs minerals, such as calcium and zinc, to maintain chemical reactions. Vitamins are important too. Each plays a very special role in our health. For example, vitamin A is used by the eyes to help with vision. Vitamin C is used by the **immune system** to help fight off illnesses and to heal cuts.

THE PROCESS BEGINS

Where's the first stop on the digestive tract? You take in food and drink through your mouth. Teeth bite and grind food into smaller, softer pieces. The mouth produces saliva, or spit, which makes food easier to chew and swallow. Saliva also contains chemicals known as **enzymes**. Enzymes begin to break food down into nutrients small enough for the body to absorb.

Once the food is small and soft enough, it's ready to be swallowed. The tongue pushes the food toward the back of the throat and down the esophagus. This is a hollow tube with muscles to propel food and drink from the mouth to the stomach.

FUN FACT

WHEN THE MUSCLES OF THE ESOPHAGUS BECOME STRETCHED WITH FOOD, THEY SQUEEZE AND PUSH THE FOOD DOWN IN A PROCESS CALLED PERISTALSIS.

How something tastes in your mouth makes a big difference in whether or not you choose to eat it.

The Five Tastes

Tiny bumps, called taste buds, cover the tongue. Taste buds help us recognize foods that taste sweet, salty, sour, bitter, and umami. Umami is a savory, brothy, or meaty kind of taste. While the tongue can recognize five tastes, the nose can recognize over 1 trillion different smells! Most of what we think of as taste is really smell, which explains why food tastes so bland when we have a cold.

NEXT STOP—STOMACH!

The next stop is the stomach. The stomach contains an extremely strong acid that helps dissolve food while also killing many types of bacteria. The stomach produces an enzyme called pepsin that breaks down proteins into amino acids.

The stomach often holds food from your last meal for hours. It slowly releases partially digested food into the next part of the digestive system—the small intestine—a little at a time. Any food that's too big for the small intestine stays longer in the stomach, where the acid and pepsin continue to break it down further. It can take foods like meat and fish up to two days to break down in the stomach!

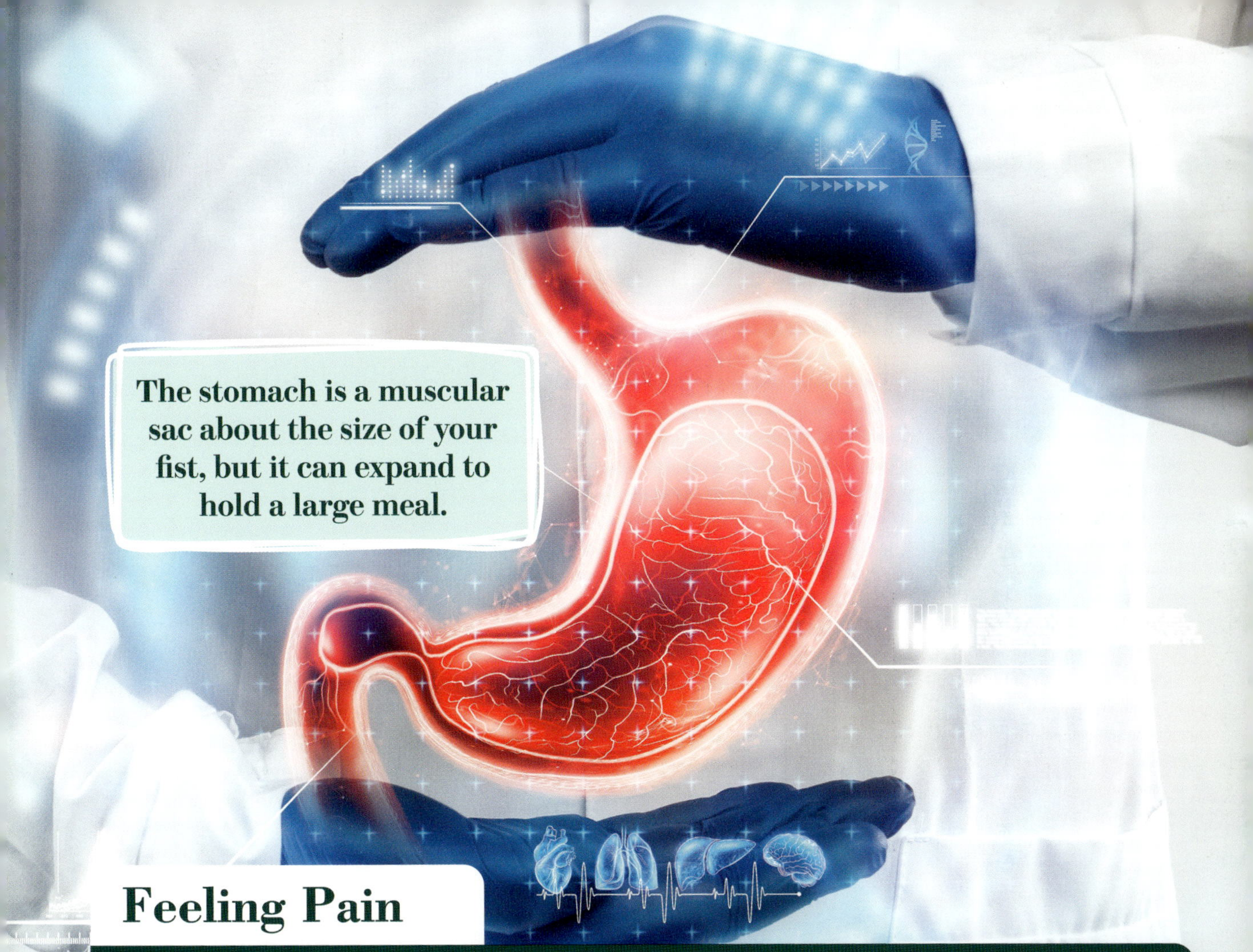

The stomach is a muscular sac about the size of your fist, but it can expand to hold a large meal.

Feeling Pain

Have you ever gotten a stomachache after eating something? Some stomach pain is from what you eat, while other pain is caused by a virus. Some people have more serious stomach pain caused by ulcers. Ulcers are small wounds in the stomach and small intestine walls that can be extremely painful. Some people suffer from heartburn. Heartburn has nothing to do with the heart. It's caused by acid escaping the stomach and entering the esophagus, causing a painful burning feeling.

ABSORBING NUTRIENTS

The small intestine has a big job—absorbing nutrients. It's called the "small" intestine because it's only 1 inch (2.5 cm) wide. However, this organ is the longest part in the human body—it's over 20 feet (6 m) long! Here, food coming from the stomach mixes with enzymes and fluids coming from the pancreas and liver. The fluids **neutralize** the stomach acids, while the enzymes finish breaking down the food into the basic building blocks of nutrition.

On the inside wall of the small intestine are thousands of very tiny, finger-like folds called villi. The villi have special channels, or tunnels, that allow the nutrients to leave the small intestine and enter the bloodstream. Villi add surface area to the small intestine to allow for more nutrients to be absorbed.

FUN FACT

THE BASIC BUILDING BLOCKS OF NUTRITION ARE AMINO ACIDS, SUGARS, FATTY ACIDS, VITAMINS, AND MINERALS.

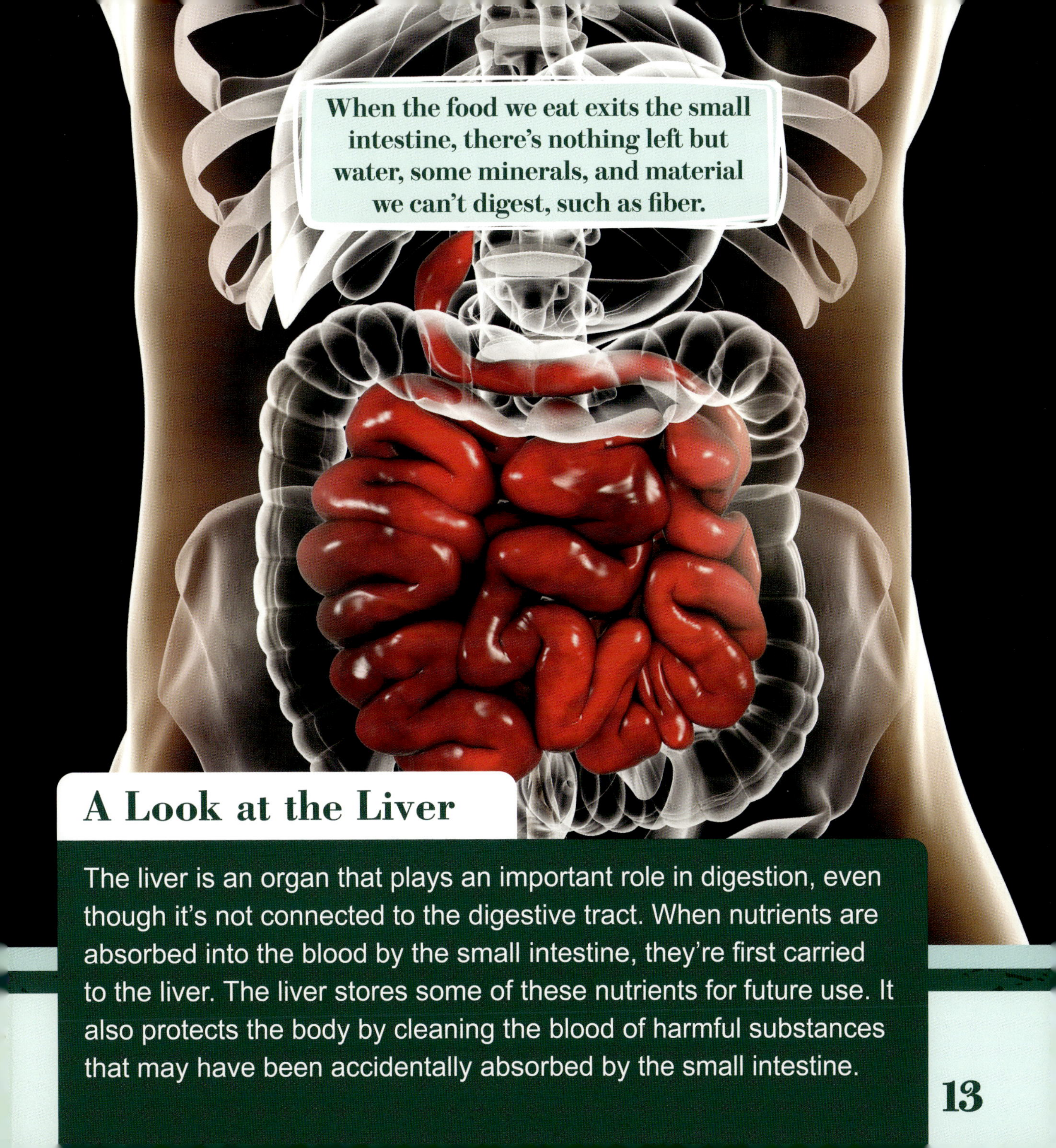

When the food we eat exits the small intestine, there's nothing left but water, some minerals, and material we can't digest, such as fiber.

A Look at the Liver

The liver is an organ that plays an important role in digestion, even though it's not connected to the digestive tract. When nutrients are absorbed into the blood by the small intestine, they're first carried to the liver. The liver stores some of these nutrients for future use. It also protects the body by cleaning the blood of harmful substances that may have been accidentally absorbed by the small intestine.

THE BREAK DOWN

The pancreas is another important organ in digestion. Many of the enzymes that aid digestion are made in the pancreas. The pancreas releases pancreatic juices, which contain hundreds of different enzymes. Each of these breaks down a specific nutrient into its basic building blocks. The pancreas is also important for producing insulin, a hormone that helps control sugar levels in our blood.

The gallbladder is a small, muscular sac that sits right underneath the liver. Its job is to store a special fluid called bile, which is a green liquid made in the liver. Bile contains special salts that help digest fats. The gallbladder can release a small amount of bile into the small intestine to help break down fat. This is useful when you eat fatty meals!

Pancreatic juices help neutralize the acids from the stomach.

FUN FACT

SOMETIMES PARTS OF THE BILE IN THE GALLBLADDER COME TOGETHER TO FORM A HARD MATERIAL CALLED A GALLSTONE. THIS CAN CAUSE A LOT OF PAIN!

AWAY WITH THE WASTE

Once the small intestine has absorbed nutrients, the next stop is the large intestine. The large intestine is twice as wide as the small intestine, but it's only 5 feet (1.5 m) long. The longest section of the large intestine is the colon. Its main job is to absorb water and minerals. About 4 pints (1.9 L) of watery material enter the colon daily, and about 3.6 pints (1.7 L) of water are absorbed into the blood. What's left is called feces, which is undigested food, fiber, and bacteria.

Feces travel though the colon the same way food travels down the esophagus and through the small intestine—by peristalsis. Normally, feces travel though the colon slowly, giving the body time to absorb water. Feces travel faster when we eat a meal.

Eating food high in water content can help your large intestine keep you hydrated.

Good Bacteria

Did you know that not all bacteria are bad? There are more bacteria in your colon than there are cells in your body! These bacteria eat undigested food in your colon and are mostly beneficial. They help crowd out disease-causing bacteria that can make you sick. Some make vitamin K that your body can use. Human feces are made up of undigested food as well as living and dead bacteria!

ON THE MOVE

What happens to waste after the large intestine is done absorbing water? The colon pushes the remaining waste—feces—into the rectum. The rectum acts as a storage area until there's a good time to let it out. This is a process known as defecation, or having a bowel movement.

Defecation is passage of the feces through the anus, which is the opening between the rectum and the outside world. Defecation is controlled by muscular rings known as sphincters. When we relax the sphincters, the feces can pass from the body. Once feces are out of the body, it's important to get rid of them and wash your hands. That's because feces is partly made of bacteria, some of which can make you or others sick.

Exercise can make feces travel through the colon faster.

The Digestive System

Use your finger to trace the path that your food takes through the digestive system.

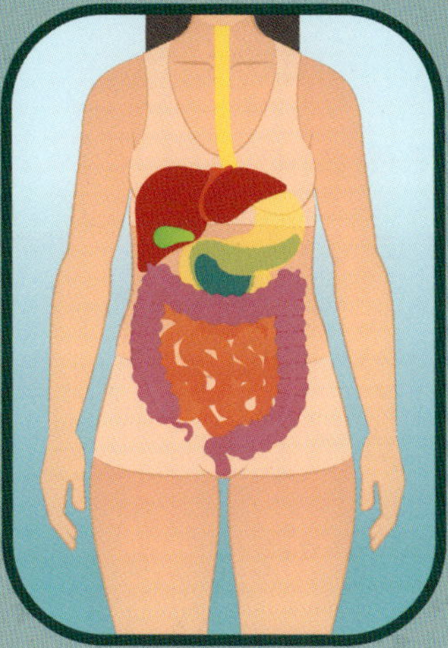

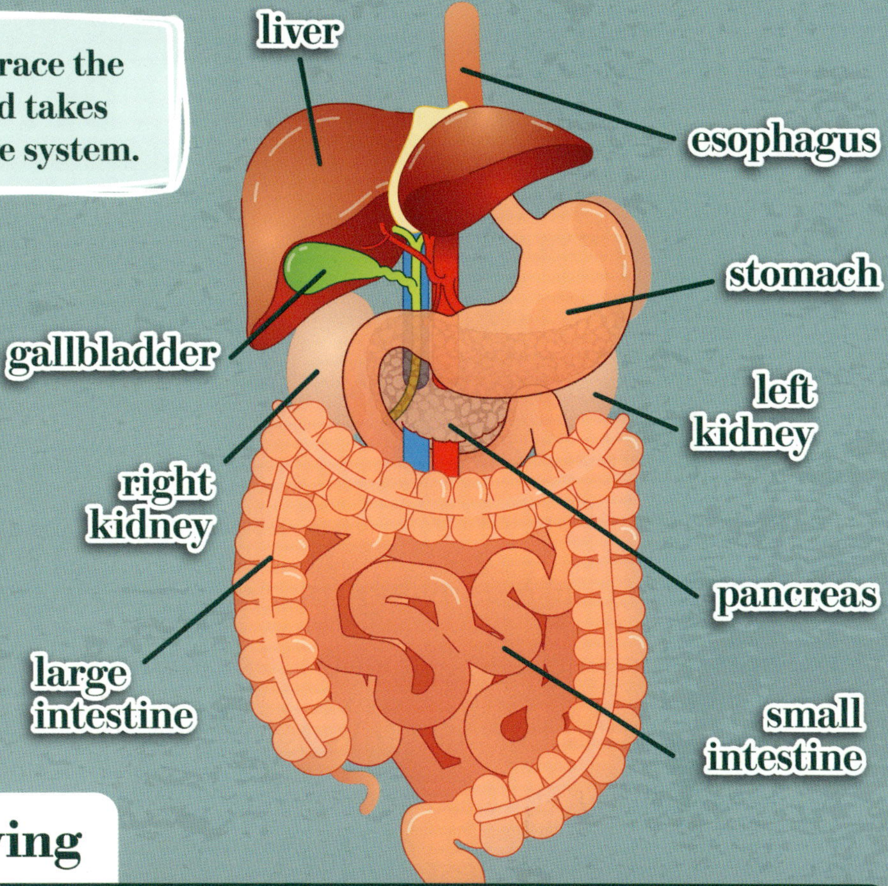

Keep It Moving

Together, the small intestine and large intestine are known as the bowel. This is where the phrase "bowel movement" comes from. When we don't have a bowel movement as often as we normally do, the feces stay in the large intestine longer, and more water is absorbed. This makes the feces harder than normal and can make defecation more painful. This is called constipation. Everyone experiences constipation at some point, but it can be prevented by drinking enough water and eating foods with lots of fiber, like fruits and vegetables.

DEALING WITH DISORDERS

Many times, your digestive system will work just fine. Sometimes, it may be thrown off by diseases or disorders. Harmful bacteria may enter the body through food and water. Stomach acid helps kill most bacteria. However, some bacteria are very hardy and can give us food poisoning, which can cause vomiting (throwing up) and stomach pain. These bacteria can live in undercooked meat, old dairy products, and unwashed vegetables.

People can also get sick when they drink water that contains germs. These germs stop the absorption of water in the colon, resulting in feces mixed with large amounts of water, or diarrhea. The body may lose a lot of water, which is why it's important to hydrate when you're sick.

Always wash fruits and vegetables before you eat them. You may be saving yourself from harmful bacteria!

FUN FACT

WATER TREATMENT PLANTS HELP KEEP OUR WATER SUPPLY CLEAN AND FREE FROM HARMFUL, DISEASE-CAUSING BACTERIA.

Abdominal pain has many causes. Appendicitis is an **infection** of a small body part called the appendix, which is located where the small intestine meets the colon. It's a pouch about the size of your pinky finger. On very rare occasions, this pouch can get blocked by feces and bacteria. The bacteria continue to grow in the appendix. Since the opening to the pouch is blocked, the appendix begins to stretch, much like a balloon. This causes very severe pain in the abdomen.

If the appendix continues to stretch, it will eventually rupture, or burst. This will spread bacteria throughout the body, making the patient very sick very quickly. Surgeons must remove the infected appendix to stop the infection. That's okay because removing the appendix doesn't harm our health.

Appendicitis stretches the appendix and causes very bad abdominal pain.

A Look Inside the Abdomen

Most of the time, you won't need surgery to find the cause of abdominal pain. Hospitals have special machines that use a method called computed tomography, or CT, to scan the body for problems. These machines take hundreds of X-rays very quickly and put them together on a computer, which allows doctors to see inside the abdomen. Many doctors use **ultrasound** machines to see images of a patient's abdomen right at the bedside.

Some people have digestive issues because they are allergic to or **intolerant** of certain foods. Lactose is a type of carbohydrate found in dairy products. For most people, lactose is broken down by enzymes found in the small intestine. However, as many as 50 million Americans are lactose intolerant. That means they can't digest lactose. This can result in abdominal pain, cramping, and diarrhea.

Gluten is a protein found in many types of flours, including wheat and rye. With celiac disease, the immune system thinks gluten is a germ and tries to attack the protein. Unfortunately, the immune system does a lot of damage to the digestive system during these attacks, which can cause abdominal pain, diarrhea, and bloating. People with celiac disease have to stick to gluten-free foods.

Allergic Reactions

Some people experience very serious allergic reactions when they eat certain foods, such as peanuts or shellfish. The immune system thinks the food is a germ, so it releases chemicals to help fight the "infection." These chemicals can do incredible damage to the body. They can cause swelling around the windpipe, making it difficult for the person to breathe. Some people are so allergic to food that they can't even be near it if someone else is eating it.

People with celiac disease often need to shop for certain gluten-free products to make sure their food has never touched gluten.

FANTASTIC FIBER

Fiber is a fantastic part of any diet. Even though it doesn't have any vitamins or minerals, fiber gives the small and large intestines something to push against during peristalsis. Without fiber in the colon, peristalsis slows down and can even stop. The longer the feces stay in the colon, the more water is absorbed, and the harder the feces become. This can make defecation painful or difficult, resulting in constipation.

Scientists also believe a diet rich in fiber helps prevent diseases, such as **diabetes** and heart disease. Fiber can be found in most foods that come from plants, including vegetables, fruits, and whole wheat. Fiber can help you keep a healthy weight. Besides making you feel fuller, fiber helps prevent the absorption of fat in the small intestine.

Beans are a great source of fiber.

FUN FACT

SOME DOCTORS SAY FRUITS AND VEGETABLES SHOULD TAKE UP HALF A MEAL. THAT ENSURES LOTS OF NUTRIENTS AND FIBER!

EAT THE RAINBOW

You may have favorite foods that you like to eat each day. However, it's important to eat a variety of foods. This ensures that you'll get enough of the nutrients that your body needs to work properly. Your digestive system can do amazing things for your body, but you have to provide it with the raw materials.

Some people say to "eat the rainbow." That means adding different colors to your meals. Phytonutrients are nutrients that give plants their color. Food from each color group can protect against certain diseases and disorders. As you take in food through your mouth, think of the ways that your body can use it. Will it give you energy? Will it help your body fight illness? Be mindful about the foods you put in your body!

Food Colors and Benefits

Red Foods

PROTECT AGAINST HEART AND LUNG DISEASE

EXAMPLES: TOMATOES, CHERRIES, BEETS, RED PEPPERS

Blue and Purple Foods

CONTAIN POWERFUL ANTIOXIDANTS, OR MATTER THAT HELPS PROTECT THE BODY

EXAMPLES: BLUEBERRIES, PLUMS, EGGPLANT

Green Foods

CONTAIN CANCER-BLOCKING CHEMICALS

EXAMPLES: KALE, SPINACH, BROCCOLI

Orange and Yellow Foods

HELP CELLS COMMUNICATE

EXAMPLES: CARROTS, SWEET POTATOES, ORANGES, CORN

Phytonutrients have many benefits. They can fight illnesses, even **cancer**!

GLOSSARY

bacteria: Tiny creatures that can only be seen with a microscope.

cancer: A disease caused by the uncontrolled growth of cells in the body.

diabetes: A disorder that causes the body to produce excess urine and causes high levels of sugar in the blood.

dissolve: To be absorbed in a liquid.

enzyme: A protein made in the body that helps chemical reactions occur.

hormone: A chemical made in the body that tells another part of the body how to function.

hydrated: Having a healthy amount of water in the body.

immune system: The parts of the body that fight germs and keep it healthy.

infection: The spread of germs inside the body, causing illness.

intolerant: Not able to eat a certain food or ingredient without getting sick.

neutralize: To make something ineffective and remove its ability to cause harm.

starch: A carbohydrate made by and stored in plants.

ultrasound: A method for seeing internal body parts using sound waves that people can't hear.

FOR MORE INFORMATION

Books

Brink, Tracy Vonder. *Digestive System.* St. Catharines, ON, Canada: Crabtree Publishing, 2023.

Hyde, Natalie. *Investigating the Digestive System.* St. Catharines, ON, Canada: Crabtree Publishing, 2023.

Mason, Jenny. *Digestive System.* New York, NY: Children's Press, 2024.

Websites

Digestive System for Kids
badgut.org/kids/
Watch videos that answer interesting questions about the digestive system.

The Human Digestive System
www.natgeokids.com/uk/discover/science/general-science/your-digestive-system/
Follow the journey that food takes through your digestive system.

Your Digestive System
kidshealth.org/en/kids/digestive-system.html
Learn all about the digestive system with KidsHealth.

INDEX